No Knowledge Is Complete Until It Passes Through My Body

ASIYA WADUD

No Knowledge Is Complete Until It Passes Through My Body

Nightboat Books
New York

ISBN: 978-1-64362-035-0

Cover art by Asiya Wadud, "Chorus Part 2," 2020
All other images by Asiya Wadud
Design and typesetting by HR Hegnauer
Text set in Sabon and Helvetica Neue

Cataloging-in-publication data is available from the Library of Congress

Nightboat Books
New York
www.nightboat.org

PART I

the order was in the hour of the workhorse

the order was
      in the hour of
            worship

the order was in the   hour of worship
      stained glass windows act as mosaic
      all radiant acts of attrition
      all foregrounded prayers supplanted
all prayers a backchannel
every pew held our bodies

we turned our bodies   to the covenant
buttressed by the Mason Dixon
and all its flat border counties

god vested his attention along its
northern border
vested his attention where he wanted
rested his attention along the crest

the only act of god   was in the hour of our worship

the cross bore
      directives
directives that could show us
shower us as a trinity
shrouds of our own making

all exemplars, prayers supplanted
all prayers supplementary work
the sun shone its piercing distance
it shone well because it wanted

the sun shone through the church
                    pew
the sun shunted us along—
the backchannel brewed

the little tight crest
began to peel at the seams
it began to gestate, it seems
as it peeled back

anything that has crossed my paths I would mother
any semblance of family   elocution,   I'm mother
all felled logic
familiar
huddled for warmth in the space between us
that's what distance does to us

this gilded foremost endeavour

                    clenched and chlorophyll
                    wrapping tendrils toward the sun

at every breath
my countenance

my long path to wholeness
no country can grant me that
my lonesome three fifths
the precise mathematics of partition
all across my selvage

                              yesterday I sat with the ocean
                              seeking out its white noise
                              held a shell up to my ear
                              settled into its subterfuge

I took a sound recording of the waves
sound waves speculation
what's with the undercurrent?
all these ocean grifters
what the flotsam water
held
in
staunch
re
lief

yesterday I rose from my bed,　　　　　Saturday morning
rode the ferry outbound
all New Amsterdam's soundless current
a polyphonic noise system
no language was staid
I broke
with tradition

h e l l o　　　　　　　　I called into a black vacuum
what I got was the virtuous salt—sonic

what I got was a reply:
　　　　　　　　　　order comes to the house of worship

I slid my fingers through the hot sand
the sun burned my right leg
I let it
the planes they flew overhead I let them
the seagulls drifted outbound
let them
all birds alight when bruised
if their wings will carry them

h e l l o   I called into a vacuous island
from the bird's eye we see   the other islands
from the bird's eye
        any light?
from the bird's eye
        pinprick?
from the bird's eye
        the sun was burning my leg I let it

I counted 17 planes
I would triple that to count the gulls
I listened to the May ocean
I was still marooned in May
I was taking flight in May
I did my day as I wanted
I was still childless
I took my time to get to the ocean
I rode the ferry lengthwise
I loved how its motor trilled
strumming us through its
cerulean backchannels

all prayers supplanted
every pew held our bodies
when we got to the waters
all the oak pews faced   the Atlantic
to carry us outbound—silt coffers
to sit with the words   held in the pews
the sun burned a hole right through me
          I let it
it was a better means
to supplant the missives

the pews got filled with our bodies
our linen garments cuff by hem by selvage
salt lined and miasma
little grains of sand embedded
how the water ebbs and the tides
bind

a few came with long rods named birches
all the branches peeled back
the order was in the hour of the workhorse

the others were in the house of worship
any small act delivers the lord's vested ships

next we managed the heap, the lumber
we dressed our hands in the lumber gloves
we used the Granberg sawmill and its guiding system
we felled the trees and trusted they'd become lumber
wasted not a single splinter
all lumber cast from selvage

diligently the Bostrichidae emerged from their
exit wounds
circular fissures in the wood's surface
we stowed inside them ardent language
undo the pestilence
smoke out the dense lattice
the dead rising right to the surface
or bet yet let them live

they built the ship's deck around us
we remained in the pews
we closed our eyes as a protective message
we cupped our hands to our ears
and amplify any noise
direct conduit to any ocean
under this pestilence the
ship's berth is coming together

during the long construction we never
rose from the pews
we knew the order was in the hour of the worship

one by one the timber became what it could become
when we open our eyes we were
on the water
the Atlantic is a matriline:
      wake
      bore hole
      wave crest
      lumber
      cadence
      incandescence
      all prayers a backchannel
      Mason Dixon bifurcated
      split along Garrett County

we touched the boat to bless it
touched all its minor parts
touched anything unruly
beyond 3/5 is the rest of Plessy
the order was in the hour of the workhorse
doused our hands in mineral oil
we blessed it, this our finished vessel
so it would shunt us far from here

no map governed our journey
the nautical chart
a rote index of possible
nexts:
       barren
       void
       electric
       language
no map yet governs us
thus no map
governs
our journey

the shrouds we tucked them in the hull

for whatever
was coming
we were to
live through it

for whatever
was coming
we were to
live with it

for whatever
was coming
we were to
live in it

we existed at the margins of the coda
we exited the ocean
all ovum rendered worthless
all ovum meritocratic
nothing else but progeny
no map yet governs us
thus no map
governs
our journey
I am etching anything
in whatever substance remains viscous

the workhorse brews to a full canter
all working hours held in accord
long hours, then longlife
countenance converge at wholeness
the numerator is filmy ocean
dividend the whole planet
all colonial demarcation
held in full credence
as if the earth existed
just to suffer this pillage

the   order   was   vested in   the   red   moon
the   order   was   in   the   hour   of   worship
how   threadbare   this   trinity —
selvage brackish   viscosity
Mason /   Dixon   covenant

the sun shines its full distance
it casts its gaze how it wants it
and what it wants is the order
of the workhorse
so what it gets is the order
of the workhorse

the honeybees invade the nunnery

grief dishevels me   my full existence
grief dishevels me every day
cobbled together—   piece by ruin
cobbled and staid, piece and filament
radiating anyway

I am trying to tell you the coastline is receding
there is grief on the coastline
there is bereavement at sea
ride the ferry the full length and you'll see

        see its compressed distance—it expels the excess coast
        all organs bear the load of our mired coasts
        all frigatebirds do this ritual when lines recede
        watch the frigatebird and see how it compensates
        it beats its wings in a slow remembrance
        it beats them long enough for the sound to fill us

the bird coasts against the demarcation but now
soars with a laden knowledge
a load is an assurance
for anything living
the load keeps us tethered, keeps us reaching—
breath by breath
plumage—gathered heap, little corners
take umbrage

I have raised my hands in the
name of tradition
I have done it twice so now it's my credence
I have done it three times so now it's a burden
this, the fourth day, my era's witness—burnished
nation state at the fifth rotation
I have raised the stakes an octave for the honeybees
to bear all their weight and the din of the wings

ride this has-been until the grid
disperses
ride all its equine parts
leave the stable   put the horse to rest
take six parts and cleave them equally
double down on familial duty
tranches act as covenant
note how the honeybees bear witness

grief, consistent across my organs
, neat restraint.
grief disperses me again—I expect it
grief—across my organs
a fastened permission
        then a willowing—
now ovum—
I told you:
        utility   and   sacrilege
        and I will try to do
        the rest

In
the
thick
of
all the
silences
(my winnowing
bereavement)
a
consistent
amber
drone
gives us
permission
to be still

If I
hadn't seen the sound
maybe it's
twilight receding
but the sameness of the
drone
pulls me—
elemental

         it grips   I follow it
         it grips what   magnet

grief dishevels me   but then there are honeybees
grief dishevels me every day
but I forgot it

cobbled together—   piece by masonwork
tibia, thorax, femur, and reaching
radiating anyway

the honeybees approach the cloister
the honeybees case the convent
their hum drowns out the nuns'
supplications
the noise enters god as a fervent
directive and god
is alive and loves the edges of
his kingdom

the honeybees thrive in the nunnery—
they know only peripheries.
as a trinity they comment on riven faith

they protect their modesty from clavicle to ulna
by shielding all their bodies' cavities
they protect their modesty with
their incandescence
and give what they will
they do and they can

on May 14
the honeybees invade the nunnery
they tag the walls
"H O N E Y B E E S were here /
we were too hungry"

when the honeybees convene we all take cover
  within the cracks of the cloister
we bore new holes
  to find a pittance of space
god will see us wherever we end
   up
god will find us whatever comes
   of us
through fence
demarcation
rough-hewn sightline
god can
see us
cresting the border

the bees bear witness to the inhabitants'
missives
they read them as the word
from Psalms to just bless us
and the ferventbees the listlessbees
plant the prayers in the garden
let them live
let them live
among such lands
as they can

    the monastic honeybees
    bless the honey
    they have learned to live
    in simple terms
    they have blessed the honey
    as a prophylactic
    against decadence and sweetness
    and all they inhabit

the honeybees invade the convent
the honeybees want the nunnery
we know their hunger we've seen
it before but we try and hold fast
to the bees as strangers

the honeybees
insist they were here all along
        we know the bees were here
        it's the fifth century of their
        drone
        any sound becomes pink noise
        all distant oceans . listen
        all calcified waters . hear them .
        any inhabitant, stranger
        inheritance as rift
        let the hive exude
        its evidence
        see how the light
        grips it?

the hive is full of xy
honeybees
humming dervishing
divining
that's living
the honeybees harbor
their modesty
the honeybees
the tonalbees the tonalbees their din
curry the claustrophobia
b ea r   witness
genuflect for better measure

                                        like me,
                        honeybees will call anything
                                              holy
                        by holy they mean that it
                        won't resist a bee's sweetness

try the bees
insist that they name
the cloistered
objects and collectively
they emit one word
for any object's name
and the word stands
in for credence
for limit
for distance
for vacuum
for all
objects within the plane
for all objects that know
no limits

the honeybees
they vacate the garden
the workerbees sweep away all
their pollinating remnants
they have worked they are spent and
are loving
——— they are guileless

the bees vacate the garden
but they encase everything
      in   honey
it's for the sake of history
we were here, that's history
a residue—that's what the bees left
which now acts as mired witness

may all deceased honeybees rest is peace
may all deceased honeybees emit a clear hum around the coast
may the bees gift us their incandescence before dying
as a final gift they supplant their wings in the garden
they do this and we have their wings—good remnants
which now acts as eyewitness, alight
which now is the migratory *I*

the garden becomes absolved and still
the amber glow quieted everything living
the nuns were in the backroom doing
their prayerful business
while the honeybees buzzed
about their heads
and the honeybees assumed
their position in the triumvirate

we assumed the bees had dispersed but
we didn't really ask them
maybe they were at rest
we never really asked them
acquiescence is a low din
we didn't have to ask them
sightline is its own knowledge
longline of honeybees
longlive honey

nationstate full of bees
nationstate amberglow
all verdant   peripheries

the nuns bustle about creating a low hum
their cheeks flush with acuity or
honey

the first nun lifts her veil for the honeybee
the bee settles into a damp spot at her neck
the bee hums and the nun is incandescent
convening with everything the bee
just made holy

more bees converge
the nun lets them in
the nun is exuberant is alive
for the living

the bees hum and sound
a low song at her nape and her god
is calmly watching near the wings
of the bees

the honey bees never called it an invasion
they called it storing their
goods
in the nunnery
they called it scaling the walls
that marked the passage
for god
and for decadence and
for all the ripe reasons

the bees lined up side by side
to pray inside the nunnery
the low hum accounted for
what the nuns wouldn't do
and they wouldn't do anything
that god hadn't
blessed
so god shrouds everything in
one fell swoop

the honeybees buzzed about the nuns' veils
this time the nuns lifted their garments
to show the bees everything:
        their brokenness
        their crises
        their sweetness
        the bees

the hive the hive
so restless with
honey

the nuns forego their shielding veils
for the sake of the honey
and if the honey touches anything
the anything is now holy
god transmutes and makes bread into
body and wine into blood
and bee into honey
and honey to nun

may god bless all honeybees
god is blessing all bees as we speak
god sits with their lone din
god is also inside it
god's logic sits with all of us
that's how he knows to bless the bees
and the bees the bees all missives
they pray   all strangers all strangers
have cloistered between us

honeybees sequestered now honeybees disperse
their diaspora a growing field   ,
their containment keeps them fervent
in the walls they bore little holes with their stingers
to look just beyond all forms of
containment

grief dishevels me not at this moment
I bore holes in the cloistered walls
that's to direct my focus

&

I have seen how the bees live   & I will live among the bees &
      the honeybees fill
any vacuous space &

                    I have seen how the bees live

chapter 2, verses 1-30
for Dionne Brand

Mexico City, 2019

vv. 1
all his five fingers were the mirror weight of the blue bird which
I cupped.
it with its broken leg
us at the end

vv. 2-3
the nailbeds & undernails yellowed & matte, what matters is
how he held the fruit—
he placed for me in a bag
the fruit
of the market
which mattered because now the bluebag
held the weight, the levied load

the bluebird limped, its blue wings an undercurrent, fluttering—
then stillness
blue in its movement
bluequiet articulation

vv. 4

I learned that if you are gentle with   a bluebird

a sparrow   a dove

they will gently double back

vv. 5-7
I removed my sweatshirt—a guardian enveloping her nest
a put the bird where it belonged

I cupped the bird in my shirt and we drove on
I slowed my breathing
the bird nested against my chest

when I asked after the smallest fruit at the market the man told me,
                                        "peel back the flesh"

vv. 8
the nailbeds and undernails carrion abutting breath
stillbird and bluebird contorting in the aftermath

vv. 9-10
the bird remained calm
the I and I called the doctor
          this is how we tended to each other:
          ████████ called the doctor, ████████ drove on

vv. 11
subsequently, I requested three of each fruit:
          three guava
          three apples
          three mandarins
          ⅓ of a bucket of the new fruit
          ⅓ of the peppers available

vv. 12
the bird tried three times to escape
each time I was humbled
by its need for flight
despite its broken
wing
each time my I
got me
I swiftly gripped back
and put the bird where it belonged
festooned in my grip
on the way to the animal doctor

vv. 13-17
outside the birds are signaling in a chorus of thirds
and then for what's to come

I left the market with the threefruit tranches
       & the bluebird in the care of the
       able doctor

sometimes I reference a picture of the bird
I have not yet pulled up the image of the bluebag with its
thirds——
it remains
evident, immediate in my proximity
this week is a way to say
that for a third of my life
I have thought about flight

            this week is to say that flight is divisible
            by three:
            action, procession, and recompense

this week is to say the visual field is a variegated membrane
with every kind of bird

vv.18
I left the market with the tranches

vv. 19-20
as I left the gentlest man, he who chose the fruit
for me, sweetly—

    or I can only know this
    kind of distributive love
    as in tending

as I left the gentlest man, he who chose the fruit
for me assuredly
took my one hand in his two hands
my hand rested, aware that I could breathe
my gaze, grace

vv. 21-25
there have been so many times where
I have sheltered birds
and in turn
where I have been
sheltered by anything

flight is the process
of ascension, a future despite absence
flight is the certain, cool vacuum of levity—this
load
we ride the air capriciously
flight attenuates to birthright

imagine all the loads we are
meant to carry
the murmurations when they finally
disperse
imagine dispersal as a series
of decisions
now dispersal as a series
of angles—

        diaspora as the low, pregnant boomerang

there have been beloved times where
I have sheltered birds
and in turn
where I have been
sheltered by whatever

vv. 26
all five fingers were the mirror weight of the bluebird which I cupped.
it with its broken leg

vv. 27
he placed for me in a bag
the fruit
of the market
which mattered because now the bluebag
tarries and waits

vv. 28

[

]

vv. 29-30
the load lightens, for breakfast I feasted from
the bluebag—
tranching the fruit out in thirds

three is anything divisible by god
a triptych is the manifestation
a trilogy is a good succession
triplets, riven ovum three times
god is anything that bears a load
a swallow is the space between my god and the bluebird
a swallow is space between my god and the bluebird

the back door or the lone coast

Abnegation began in December   something to
do with the raw nature of endings—to do with saline clarity
or finish. Abnegation or I can have it both ways—as in part
credence part self-splayed   the heart line of my left
palm extends to receive whatever it is you place in it.
I bet it will be sustenance because I have known how it is to be fed

abdication or the act   of annexing another country or
the act of crawling deeper into the hole for the purported days
 that act as some extension

I made a charcoal line in   the wet cement while it
was being laid, stuck a few pebbles in the corner as the cement
set. Knew each time I saw   the pebbled surface
would be reminded of the moment when   I placed the
pebbles in the pavement of the wet cement

        I am always half here moving the bouquet around the
            house, let its little shuddering petals fill me
    hold the neck of the vase   don't dare let it slip

abnegation began in December   something to do with the
self-made endings

chlorophyll in the winter is a commitment but possible—train
the pothos towards the sun so that it can also grow
might as well let it grow if you plan to let the plants live.
I could not burden you with this kind of abnegation so instead
took to the bed—stayed there all night
slept for the eight hours of it, woke up on a Saturday

my head leaked the message   everything set to orchestra pitch

the radio reminded me that if I could commit I could do it my way
place my foot in the black asphalt take my foot to the cement for
clearance

the cooler weather began in December I didn't notice when the
cloud coverage ended—my eyes were trained on the ground and
since I trained them I saw the   phalanx of my winter shelter

in the night I sweat out all the abject days   or
humiliation the ceiling fell around me
and I belatedly sought shelter under the
desk   I asked my sister to join me   and I awoke at the
threshold
snowbanter of drywall   dreamlike in this way
I awoke at the threshold—all cleave and cleft

abnegation is a coolish lean lake   slipping into the logic
of three fold then deliverance
the hull marks its own shape   the hull marks its own shape

abnegation is an aseptic aqua lake   I have seen this
kind of water   all stylized and brute   all
shelter shorn and brute all gradient, stalled becoming

I have seen this kind of water   leaks out to life
something like a crosshatch
but I think he said we are only   made by giving away what
humble placeholders we are given   and what we are given
was cultivated in a garden
Arkansas crosshatch   cane crawl down the corridor   faith talk
and myrrh or iron ore and oxidation

I have tried to board a flight   bird-like and furcula—wishing and
my documents. Night train and terror—compartments or gardens
I have tried to board a flight   I succeeded 78 times
Stamp marked my entry   foul language my exit
but anyways means nothing to me—barely matches my imprint
I retreat to the garden—let its language provide   the slippage
let its countervalence
get more vivid   let to let to let to lean

between Christina Sharpe & Torkwase Dyson:
what kind of space would you need to move 500 people quickly

I have used the blueprint as   a maritime future   used it as a
seafaring fold
all foul futures never rest—blueprint I'll show the magistrate
and expect to claim what is mine or at least clarify what I meant

I thought to ask permission or to just erase the door from the
back entrance
room to room to room to green finish   vaunted ceilings and
picture windows

a vacuum or comfort in the cavity comforted by the room and
oiled all the birch doors
abnegation or the lone coast the back door or the lone coast
clarify what I meant or the lone coast

PART II

proviso for asphodel fields

Meanwhile, the clouds are white and the sky is all blue.
Why so much god. Why not a little for men.

Clarice Lispector, *The Hour Of The Star*

quietude, gaped earth, substantial loss

the ferries encumber their own weight. they pass each other at close range. the unlikely vessels transmit their cargo. all the bodies carry on. everyone on board is black. everyone covets a faithful salvage. the carrion circle overhead. they patiently stake out the rippling time. then time shirks us and newspapers yellow. time evidenced in furled edges. I wanted to hold their full weight in my palm. palm is plan spelled oblong. the plan was to meet in the Alpujarras, work the farms til our good bones yellowed. work the earth til it shone gold black. we note the slippage of time. the spilling vessel, the elastic edges. the lax maps. the precedent. they establish the changing need: less fuel, pack the vessel, reference the Middle Passage etchings for knowledge of how the ship is packed. how the threads rope us into a seamless package: quietude, gaped earth, monumental loss. the crisp cutting siren of the new day dawning. the shoreline with its subtleties and the mirror image that we name *this duty*.

the spilling vessel, the elastic edges. the lax maps. the precedent. we cut our losses—we named them knowledge we came back heavy we reached for the narrows. we lived in yeses and gracious miracles. meanwhile, in our mourning: islands remember everything, that's how they subsist immemorial. they carry on hopeful that the archipelago remits light. the island searches out the light, and it is easy to find when you're primed for looking.

we trusted in the cutting sea. subcutaneously we are gold. our livers are fatty. our lungs contain the dense, unkempt air. the mandible cuts fear. the ulna refracts elastic edges. the wave frequency extends aeternum. I intend to measure the distance. we all supplicate and keen. we all supplicate and cup an exacting distance.

the boats pass each other at close range. I count 77 bodies. 77 shoulder girdles abutting the wind. the unlikely vessels disgorge their cargo. colony and agony rhyme in duress. all the bodies carry on. I must confess the carrion circle overhead. when time passes, newspapers yellow. the obituaries name a weighted coffin. the lives never lose significance. we were born, each of us manifold, and that's how we'll die, too, subcutaneously gold.

the edges furl to show where time waned. I wanted to hold their full weight in my palm. palm is plan spelled oblong. the plan was to meet. Palermo anciently slips with the tides. the spilling vessel, the elastic edges. the lax maps. the precedent. how the threads rope us into a seamless package: quietude, gaped earth, monumental loss. the crisp cutting siren of a day delivering. the shoreline with its subtleties and the alkaline duty, equally of self and of a distant progeny.

quietude, gaped earth, monumental loss

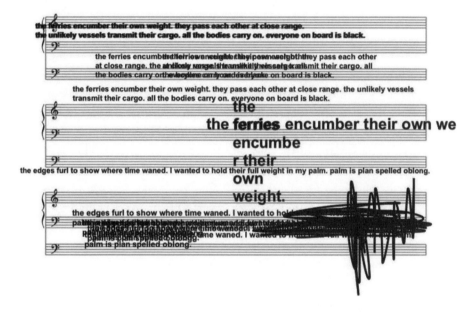

the ferries encumber their own weight. they pass each other at close range. the unlikely vessels transmit their cargo. all the bodies carry on. everyone on board is black.

the ferries encumber their own weight. they pass each other at close range. the unlikely vessels transmit their cargo. all the bodies carry on. everyone on board is black.

the ferries encumber their own weight. they pass each other at close range. the unlikely vessels transmit their cargo. all the bodies carry on. everyone on board is black.

the
the ferries encumber their own we
encumbe
r their
own
weight.

the edges furl to show where time waned. I wanted to hold their full weight in my palm. palm is plan spelled oblong.

the edges furl to show where time waned. I wanted to hold their full weight in my palm. palm is plan spelled oblong.

on the structure of birds

Can you read a map? Who taught you that the good north was that? Can you spell *fatal* to map an abiding passage? The fata morgana is always superior. It senses the horizons and it laps the waters. Who taught you to read the map like that? Can you see the map? You mean the manifested frontier? Can you see it like that? I know what I saw and he was contrite. I know what I saw and the other was holy. All the many ways of seeing. Who taught your English? And who taught you like that? Who named you and said come straight to the light? What goodness, what many Wolof men still think Rio holds some dream? What northern light, who sees Cherifa and only then sees Jane? Who sees light streaming in from my fourth floor garret? This is a suitable abundance, this clasp I call sun. This is some newness I'm catching to rectify the loss. Who told you this semblance should be named language? Who wrought this, some small god lingering in stillness, some prophet twice disposed, some dirty fingernails, some of the ransacked. Who told you once bitten now the baby's shy? Who likes a god who dreams in total and wide? I've left for today so I can come back strong. Who knows the word *borders* is a foul translation for brethren? Who knows the map is better left dead? Who told you that? Who speaks through a knotted tongue? Whose pine needle branches? Who would say the swallow slopes its four chambers to the sun? Who would say the swallow's furcula breaks in two? Who two would say that a freebird freely alights? Who then would say a freebird enters any nation? Who knows the freebird can eat any worm? The freebird keeps no army and is not bellicose. Who wants to look me in my face and remind me daily that I come from small hands. Clean hands. Clay hands. And mired hands. I learned by rote to read a map. Noting the islands and the passage, the pillaged and the damned. How they all erode with time. The north star and the expanse of dry heat. Fine sand. Who dares to say that a whole people are not a desire line? Bahia fits into Douala's neat cove. Who unfolds a long shrift before the patera's even left? Who hopes that a benign but mighty force quakes us? Who prays for Palermo and prays in pidgin? Who speaks what they need and gives grace in a patient tongue? Who has no mother and thus no mother tongue? Who needs Lampedusa when an isthmus is willing? Who needs an isthmus when both ends reach to nothing? Who needs the nothing when the map is not prophetic? Can you read a map? Who taught you the good north was that? Who never told you where our kin licked the flame? Can you read a map? Who told you it was written in our tongue? Who named you and said come straight to the light? Who named you, they said come straight to the light.

See the schism

See the schism and know that it can no longer hold water. From the other side I don't reach for you, I pull you. I see that your palm is open and I grip it carnivorously.

I reckon, a latitude
{between Tripoli and Lampedusa, there is nearly the Gulf of Sidra}

you feel pretty perilous. you'd rather perish in the water than
languish near Tripoli's sullied edge. you are changed, your lids
hang heavy, straight through the sanguine. all through the sinew.
the sea beckons and wakes you. a natural death is understated.
you cut the tide with exactitude. You cut it with a calm light and
you're boundless in the sea, and lifted, too. cut the waves and quell
Sidra's doom. The gulf between us elemental and the surest route
to Lampedusa is iron salt and oxygen. You name the sea to rise
and meet it and put to rest Sidra's obstinance.

Your doom—if anything—would be Sidra, Sidra would ensnare
you. Reel you in by lifeboat only then to anchor you. Your light is
rightly steadfast and honed. You insist on a precision, recalling the
instructional manual: the breaststroke is a leisurely way to pass
through the narrows. You insist and are decisive, count the breaths
exactly: 2 for every 1 for the damned and the saved.

but then, too.

the miasma of petrol and saline pocks you. some perish nameless.
we search out the remaining phosphorescence. starboard remains
keen and searing. near the satisfied edge. your stroke became
heavyweight. port is increasingly distant. the dread is manifold
it needles, incandescent. a refuge is the voyage the labor is the
passage the coming is the collapse the crusade of the Sahara.
The desire line snakes irregularly. the steady traffic pauses. we
enumerate the loses. we harbour the living and we know all it
means to carry their weight.

we begin the task of naming them all. incanting them in a
coming fugue. invoking them to ward off Sidra. naming them as
a prophylactic. the milieu of the how to canter on, each footfall
anew, the archipelago that names the state

others come others onward.

[a vessel remains] [the onward, itinerant] [the engine, they lift]
[I reckon we're remnants] [Sierra Leone] [a latitude, we name it]

an equivocation along the illuminated coastline. Libya of the
bygone—is an insistence. you gesture with exactitude. You cut
the waves with a calm light. you're burnished, and lifted, too.
a wide, high heat stayed near you, all through the passage, all
through the mooring.

the gaping sea beckons and breaks you. the impotence the
imploring the inured. the inexact. the crisis. the crease. port is
increasingly distant. you ache for a semblance of. the vantage of
this one. the proliferation. they are out of sight until they are a
sightline. black coal as ravens weightless as gold plovers marshal
the waters my dear Crosslight, feast on your plentiful oxygen.
starboard is penetrating. port, sagacious.

you can say you were pretty perilous.

you didn't languish near Tripoli's sullied edge. you are changed,
all you bears the blackness all you bears the possible goldness.

straight then sanguine.

it was satisfactory

venus was humbled. the heat too high. the light was satisfactory. The air sanguine. The life right. Everything exceptional. The heat was formidable. The angle was not my own. The night sky was doomed. The ruin was total. The sky or blaze. I'd like to be your dearest kin. I'd like the seam to envelope me. My life is a clean clam. The light becomes more claustrophobic. The border sears the burden. The acuity too grand. The light won't diminish the night remains decadent. We numbered the stars. All among them. The brightest. The burnished. The bleak. The deleterious. The delicate. The deliberate. The daunted. The destitute. The dervishes. Venus was humbled. the heat was too high. the light was satisfactory.

A phoenix or again this ruin

The brutal is etched but the bird alights. The brutal is written but the bird alights. The brutal is engraved but the bird alights—

Take flight stay right but the bird alights. Take flight stay right but the bird alights.

PART III

yucca brevifolia: field notes from an ellipse

1. This morning I learned that the frigate bird sleeps on average twelve seconds while in flight. Its wings continuously beat and it perseveres on its journey, as flight and sleep are not mutually exclusive occurrences for this creature. Its red plumage billows to burst, the velveteen blood red, pristine sunsets at its breast.

2. He props up the camera and takes a series of long exposures. The shots are atmospheric; the wide, barren, plundered night sky is cut only by the sudden red rock that juts this way and that, some sharp angles, some wavy, lasting curves, some snaked spines. It all looks like mars and I marvel: how did he do that? How did he show us what the sky did not even hold?

3. Every week, I religiously sit with my mother tongue. I come home from my post at the library, where I lead a conversational English class. We break to the bones the nuance of inflection— try to get right the intent. Someone asks "Is there a difference between *last*, *lust*, and *lost* in pronunciation? I cannot see it." No one understands me, they lament, and they mistake my *last* for *lust* and my *lust* for *lost*.

I turn squarely to them and point to my open mouth. Say *last* and fifteen voices all say *last*—I draw out the short a. Say *lust* and again the voices. Now say *lost*. They do. *Last. Lust. Lost. Last. Lust. Lost.* Everyone laughs at these three subtleties. My pregnant wife lusts for many foods, Arman offers. *This is the last stop on this train*, they all know from riding the train. We joke that it is the lost stop. Or the lust stop. I train myself to speak slowly and with sharp diction.

4. I learned that the northern wheatear makes a transatlantic flight—migratory creature from eastern edge of the Atlantic to western shores. What does a northern wheatear revere enough to tuck under its capable wing in flight, carrying essentials from east Atlantic to west Atlantic?

5. We gather around the dinner table every Wednesday night, a confetti of colors, the dead and dying ranunculus obscuring my direct line of sight. I recount my favorite moments of English conversation, such a language to relearn.

6. After the surgery, through the fog of the painkillers, I hear you with the green gooseneck watering can making the rounds from dracaena to pothos back to the dracaena, trimming this one and pruning and training that one toward the sun. Sometimes you enter the living room and gaze out at the plant world, them growing in their many greens. Yucca brevifolia you say. Yucca brevifolia I repeat. I sink back into a replete fog.

7. My eyes are closed and I'm heavy with my own thoughts. I hear the tinkle of the watering can. The plants seem to require so much these days. I could have sworn you just watered them all not two days ago. You are attentive and pluck anything not living and train the pothos.

8. Now the desert is parched and the earth is barren and there are no sounds except the open piece of the wide sky, the narrow road stretches along indefinitely. I'm at the wheel. I'm driving. I know the brake from the gas. I don't kill anyone. I don't drive us headlong into a truck. I motion to something on the side of the road and the steering wheel lurches for a second. I jerk it back and keep my eyes on the road. I close my eyes and brace for a head-on collision. The truck wavers towards me in the high desert heat and wind—and passes. Whooosh of the wind. We pass the truck. Whooosh. And everyone is still alive.

9. The Upper Great Highway is dusted in a quite fine film of sand and the high, steep dunes block the view of Ocean Beach. The dunes are pocked with delicate, little red ice succulents, growing improbably there among the sand, its rootwork shallow. Here I learn to drive along this highway. The air is still—approachable and inviting. The sky—a simple and unbroken blue. Along this stretch of the highway is my favorite place as of late, the lone restaurant along this piece of the road, a restaurant with a big WPA mural on the ground floor and a second floor full of picture windows that look out onto the Pacific Ocean. I come here alone sometimes.

Here in the parking lot, Annette, my driving teacher, pops open the driver's side door and I grip my passenger side handle, forever ambivalent about driving. Asiya, you can do a lot of things and you can do this, I tell myself. Most people drive and so can you. This is a highway at a finisterre, something I love.

10. Years later, an ellipsis of time: I google image a canoe and see many men, lean and strong, all syncopated with their angular arms. Back and forth and and back and forth propulsion in the free ocean. You request a picture of the tree village we created. I ready the house, making neat piles of all the overflow books that line the coffee table.

11. I train the pothos. I dutifully train the pothos's long, tired limbs. I drape a leafy arm over my shoulder, angling myself to the upper reaches of the window and away from the light. I push a pin into the wall there and rest some pothos, gingerly, atop the pin. I place another pin further down the wall. I've put this off for seven months, watching the pothos sigh and heave under its own winter and spring and summer weight. Sorry, I say, turning my back to them.

12. Topiary, you taught me, at Winterthur. Hmmm. Look at all the comical shapes—some human did this. You'll stare up at the sun, crinkle your nose and look at me head-on. Topiary, you'll say. That's the name for the conical, comical bushes formed into tidy shape. That was in Winterthur.

13. Again: this morning I learned that the frigate bird sleeps, on average, twelve seconds while in flight. Its wings continue to beat and it perseveres on its journey, as flight and sleep are not mutually exclusive occurrences for this creature, its red plumage billow to burst, the velveteen blood red, pristine sunsets at its breast.

PART IV

Leave something to be built

1. *(if) Some houses in the town of Baarle-Hertog/Baarle-Nassau are divided between Belgium and the Netherlands. At one time, according to Dutch laws, restaurants had to close earlier. For some restaurants on the border this simply meant that the customers had to move to a table on the Belgian side*

2. *(then) The trophoblast is made up of an internal layer of cubical or prismatic cells...and an external layer of richly nucleated protoplasm devoid of cell boundaries*

if, after birth the border

You can live with the paradox. You can see how dispensable the day is. How a father can entrench his own son how a good god can yoke everyone. we dispense light for the sake of seeing. we dispense it for seeing the muted and the incandescent. I placidly await the light that will change me. this equanimity and any of the gathered can be the light to the summit. we define the path as we proceed and note all other precedents. the possibility refracts all the light. the desire path and the faultline. you can live with the paradox. a wish to demarcate where the switchback finishes. we call out to whomever is listening: I am here, how can I be?

we are born so porous, trusting in our able membranes and the bright sacristy that envelopes us. We live with the paradox insisting the levee, insisting the breach: shore and where it meets the accosted land. fire and where the sand cuts the flame, the oak, and from where the variegated leaf springs. a sheep and when it brays to meet the day. the breaking work of the aleph and the zed. the whitest hope and where it shirks the sea. the cumulus and the litmus test. we live with the paradox. the wall is on both sides; there is depravity of mind. We are listless, stagnate, reaching, marshaling the waning time. we spent all this time seeking sustenance for our eventual cell walls. the vantage that shows us what we need to carry on, the assumption that we would do it alone. if, after birth, a border then. if, after birth, the chorion is ephemeral. the many villi neatly come with a trophoblast's revelry. let's say the trophoblast is devoid of cell boundaries. we are born so porous trusting in our able membranes. and then we devote the next century to our selfsame cell walls.

if/then. if, after birth, we live with the paradox. after birth we can seek the Baltic, the North Sea, or the Bay of Biscay. If, after birth, rather Banjul, then harken the trophoblast's frontierless dawn. if/then Molenbeek, Dearbord, Almeria, Santa Barbara's low sun we sought. the day is indispensable, which helps us live with the paradox. we dispense light for the sake of seeing in the dark. we expect the earth to turn so that it delivers our assemblage. all through our reaching. at the ever if/then. we dispense light to burnish the dark. it is possible to live with any paradox.

the atoll of my great country
[redefining the terms]

atoll
/ˈatɒl,əˈtɒl/

verb

> protect, fortify, build up, wall off, confidently proceed
> with limited knowledge, onward, establish (political)
> precedence

1. How to use it in a sentence:

   a. *We thought it safer to atoll ourselves than face,
      head on, the uncertain future.*

atoll
/ˈatɒl,əˈtɒl/

noun

> The rapid transformation of a once giving nation into
> one governed by a latent fear, bred from a presumed,
> imminent threat. Nation states in atolls preemptively
> insulate themselves by building walls of increasing
> heights. The goal is for no one to see out/need out and
> for no one to see in/come in.

2. How to use it in a sentence:

   a. *Where once existed contiguous, open landforms,
      we now have mostly atolls.*
   b. *After sailing the perilous seas for the night, they
      arrived at land only to realize it was an atoll.*

archipelago

/ˌɑːkɪˈpɛləgəʊ/

noun

The assured acknowledgement that all islands emit light and all landforms are capable of receiving them. The archipelago acknowledges the dire state of being, and thus fortifies its knowledge by seeking out other islands beyond its knowing. The notion that other islands have answers too buoys the archipelago. For the past many centuries, the various islands of the planet's many archipelagos have gotten on well, despite their being no walls. There is an open invitation for atolled nations to seek out archipelagos.

1. How to use it in a sentence:

    a. *The archipelago knowledge that ties the islands are lit with an ascendant light.*

concerning the house I stayed in, December 2017

it was a house of approximations, the veil so thinly—the doors
opening at their obtuse angles; a bit contrite, constructed
and laid bare, reconstructed for a futile era. it was a house of
approximations, one where a body laid bare was a mute object.
the windows also called barronesses, the windows encrusted,
apt for this season.

it was a house of approximations, one whose mother tongue
demanded nothing, one whose father was so liminal and who
held a tight grip even through the final flight.

the house, a coterie, a valence of primer-and-paint-in-one
good enough to map newness and   the white frailty
in the void.

from this vantage the foundation was becoming, proportioned,
brick, patently partitioned, blanketed

a building made of ███████████.

we could say the   well, by way of fire exit   the

house of approximation   is just as good as any.

we set them out across the channel

the window was a clean compass
our loving instrument due north, and
the exit was so narrow—
that was to direct our focus

                                 when we got
                                 north we found
                                 the hollow

and when we found the hollow
we didn't lament
it was a matter of expectation
that we would need to
examine the blueprint
with precision and then
we'd scrap it

we gauged and
cradled the monk's rest
I mean
together we decided to
cobble something wrought from
what we had in plentitude
what we had in common:
marrow, alabaster, a throughway, a glove

we weren't scared
when night came
with everything it envelops
the moon readily exerted—

the tide
        grew
we took shelter where we could
really just inside each other

we each held each other
just long enough
to imprint
marrow alabaster
warbler
glove

we considered the northern
wheatear stayed in its
sightline
knew when its wings folded
it was time for us to crest
too

transmigratory or
just the everyday diasporic
pedestrian in the fact that we
now have to name this

the hollow was electric
in its sameness
in the fact
that each turn
elicited something
newly hewn

the metric was what
can we call porous?
and what has transmuted
for too long that
it didn't find its way home

on Wednesday we made
paper cranes
we set them out across the channel
they were a bit cautious and
they were lovely in their
fates

and when we found nothing
we didn't lament
it was a matter of expectation
that we would need to
examine the blueprint
before we could ever ingest it

we put on the market a
detached single
family home
each room held a border
in every wall there was
a
holding
pattern

in the broader rooms we
held each other, right before we
sent ourselves out across the
fissured channel

     *

I left the warbler's door
ajar I knew I'd need to peer
in, the little mystic
guiding us
in all its teeming
immanence

At first, day one

take the table
take the book

take the cup

       the object, animated
       the object, mute

don't drop it
don't drop it
       be it cylindrical
       oblong
       in a hurry
       quiet

place it
  next to your body
and then
notice every
           body in the space
           every
                 body's itinerant object and
                 ownership, may always be tenuous

           train your silence to fill the space
           your even breathing, switchback
           if your eyes and your tongue will let you

move with them and
        and
        and in them, then
move with them and
move the table
        by fortitude, forfeiture, or by carrying it
think of it as one large plane—made manifest
in which anything can become
        whatever
set the glass there and it leaves its daylong   water-ring.
                                                     halo.
                                                     O.
                                                     marking.
                                                     object.
                              obscene what it needs to leave.

but
don't drop it
don't drop it
        mute magic
        fissured moment
        tangle island

I need the clock to ferry the hour
the cloaked minutes become
their own resolute tables
        sliding everything against or at each other

know your body
know the distance
what have you

the bric-brac

whatever

before
everything
continues, slides nearly collapses

                        this is day one
                        or this is day one
                        and this is day one.

I am willing to
use my feet

I am willing to try for
            extension
ask for it—now extend

now take the object
take your two hands
take the book

don't drop it

use your eyes
triangulate the movement, fine focus
fixed futures

use your hands
if you are able

take the cup
      or
      book
            or

backpack
container

horizontal arrangement
flagrant
          bouquet
take it
take it all and then

                    place it at the center of our table

we know your name, our eyes said
we know your name, our mouths said
we know your name, our eyes said

in aggregate we say your name

                    assume your goodness
                    assume your goodness
                    assume your goodness

our feet bear the burden
in the atrium
as we approach the table
and again as we disperse

                    *

in our lives we can notice a breath,
          then breathing

house series 5

every year my body fails me
like some ship at half mast
I am not exceptional
every
            body does this

circling what's null then
some narrows
passing through the little
places

slipping everything aside
my body is worse off
than I remember

                    a container ship—
                    pound for pound   does the loving
                    eschews anything called distance
                    insists on how it will
                    train the unruly edges

every ocean or a body
say water
every curved limb say
logic
every filmy ocean say veils me
starboard over
mother tongue
patriline for white lies

all my organs
passing time in iodine and saline
waters passing on when
their use is spent
some organs fulgurated
all this logic levied

a container ship—
pound for pound   does the loving
kindly hosts anything called distance
insists on how it will blessedly
train the unruly edges

all my organs
subsisters
passing on when
their use is spent
some organs fulgurated
all this logic evident

all my organs
an entanglement
all my vantages estrangements
every year my body
encloses
one fewer organ

I will never escape my poverty
my plentitude in dearth
no matter my ascent
my body carries its own
mathematics
my lodestar does
its duty

every year my body's frailty
like some ship circling
a thin space
I am not exceptional
every
          body does relent
the gale, the void then the narrows
passing through the little
places
slipping everything aside
my body is fine

I remember
a container ship
does the loving
eschews anything called
distance
insists on the patchwork,
organdome
how it can't
train any edges

I have thought about the oven
as a way to conduct heat
thought back to the equator as a means
to an end

I have thought about the ovum
as a way to consecrate heat, next
progeny
thought back to the equator as a means
to slate time
thought back to the time to when a little
slip gripped me
clawing and needling and needing and needing

every year my body does a distance,
distributive—like some ship at half mast
I am not exceptional
every
body does this

PART V

attention as a form of ethics

We are mired in matter until we are not

—Ralph Lemon

attention as a form of ethics

let's dissect what it means to mourn
let's look at all the desiccant and what's left
little exoskeleton bareback
how the straight line can become apparent
how the likeness is a labile breeze

let's talk about shame
            and my face
look at my kneecaps
            my eyelids
let's talk about hailing cabs
let's look at my map
look at how you molded me
I was a smattering of young kudzu

look at the vagrant earth
see what you see when you look
                when you say *see*?

how the curvature becomes apparent
each vertebra the catacombs
cat scratch and hay fever
little motor at my shoulder

let's round up the dead
the ones with the quick shuffle
the droopy sole, the double knot high tops
let's look at the country
call it territory as we're still
deciding
the green heap how it was electric
let's look at the spectral
to see how you molded me, I was a little sweetbriar

let's be discreet when we claim this
wouldn't want to tempt them
myriad crystal landforms
each silent as the ocean

now look at my topography
now look at the mountain range
how can we ever do it justice?
do you know how we can do it justice?

I have a keen aphasia
I call it code switch
it's
kept
me
alive
how I can be anything? I'm
shaped only in the dialectic

everyone has their own pride
lions move with mute magic
some animals are nocturnal
and some mother orcas mourn

I thought we were an archipelago
each felt under our own expanse of gilded wing
let's make an assumption
let's make an assumption that   the lake has a bottom
let's make an assumption   that everyone will mourn
let's sack a hundred greenbacks
for the sake of acknowledging they mean something
what does it mean to have worth?
who would dream to drain a lake?

I spent my days staring into the eye of the Baltic
it's because I am also a body of water
it's not that onerous
I've built a muscle memory
it's not that heavy

let's talk about erasure I mean
that's easy
start with a word that you don't like
start with a people you didn't know
start with a neighborhood, rank
start with any miasma dispersed

let's talk about burden
let's talk about burden for the weight
it lends us
let's talk about supplication
about my palms—uplift, patience

let's celebrate our substance
subsistence in
amber rivulets of stilllife
constellations how you molded me
country how we became it
the longitude is a contested border
my longest muscle I named familiar

let's reckon with the past
the logic
the Middle Passage
the hull
the tenderness
you are such demanding work

let's demean what we don't like
because it's easier than a reckoning
let's say the past means that it's finished
never acknowledge how it throbs
immutably
forever finishing its punishing business

let's talk about observance
          pistils
ugly shapes
let's talk about all the demands
let's talk about mediocrity
let's spell it wrong
let's talk about a quick conversation
one that skims the waters, a little stream
downcreek
let's talk about weariness

I'm all about my brokenness
I mean I'm all about let's disperse
there are countless vessels and I rode them
there is a church door and it's open

let's get silky
let my cat connect with me
let the window stay a little open
let my lids stay open

don't call me labile
it's normal
for everything to move
just like any ocean

you didn't make a language
you made a few fissures
you made a little rucksack
you got down on your knees and called
this patchwork pilgrimage

let's remove the obvious from the image
what's left the residue
history is so residual
what's left the spectacle
what's left the spectral
a magnolia tree ransacked
the south is its own dispersal

I'm not afraid of the dark now
see its throbbing transmission—see its blackness
see its breath in fog, Ines
and then it comes into focus

most knowledge is scant magic
don't let me forget my language
don't mistake umbrage for a coffer
matte for high yellow
and, too, this gold

I have trouble with I
     I am the valley   I am the hill   I am a ravine
     I am gaping   I am foxglove
I am both
nightshade
and
mourning

I have troubled I
I bore bronson
I bore brownstone
I bore down on the bit left
pillage and all that
with a quickness doubles back
made an urgent isthmus

let's talk about age 9
about what we used to know
the magic, the marvel, en punto.

you can't force justice
must move at the jaundiced pace of history
the gaping circularity

you must force justice
move against its low tide
all the things it jettisons
the politeness of collateral damage
must move from the jaundiced
pace of history
the gaping circularity

        let's write something to quiet us
        call it pernicious in the valley
        aerate the soil for old time
        palm oil for the propulsion

I have loved from a great distance
from manifold mired treatments
little tree rings that barely reach
up the foxglove down the cove

let's talk about elegies
        dirges
        drifting,   snow caps
        peat moss   and stillness

what is a quiet kingdom?
what dim band of light?
what is my birthright,
my comportment?
what is my breedlove?

what is the expanse before
          I bore witness?
what is a country without a crest?
plaster instead of greatness
manifest in lieu of recompense?
what is the creed that keeps us?

let's tumble toward my kind of south
barrel through the mid atlantic
hate on all its confinement
long for a few restrictions
cultivate the overtures

                    the magic
                    the marvel
                    a new form: the moonbridge

let's make a meal and call it supper
butter the bread and call it finished
high tide for latitude
low tide for night swim

let's dissect what it means to mourn
let's look at all the desiccant and what's left
how the straight line becomes branded
how the likeness is a labile breeze

let's talk about shame
let's talk about my face
look at my kneecaps
let's talk about nail beds
let's look at my map
can't be used as evidence
by tomorrow we are
drifting
with our coffers
and by daybreak
you will have had
me molded

PART VI

There is a room

choral or

choral   or   multiple
        or   continental
                        or   fibonacci
or   rest here or
                                notice the marriage
                                of plentitude and then

choral or
        fabric and selvage
                slither slather
                        and honeycomb
or   convent   and
        bridge   or   weft and
stray language for sentence
their long years   assume
their business

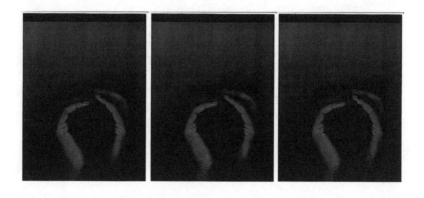

choral   or took   to
       the   bed   or
       gathered up the blankets tucked
    anything inside primed it for music

took   to
       the   bed   or
       my
hands cupped to contain   the clean   water
       or   just   rest
here

choral or
       frail lattice   and   frayed ligature
       or gathered isthmus
my faulty dependence
or   grip   so now   the hands are
covenant

       choral or muted
muted or slippage
       three points or threadbare
    threadbare and chanting
in   agreement

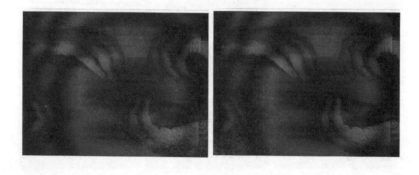

choral or
      we have said what we said
           at dawn then later the same thing said
to etch the choral the marvel the
gangway

         the storm
                    the   shed
        inside the manual
work or
        multiple
        continental
        fibonacci
        or   rest here or
        notice the marriage
        of plentitude and then

Straight Lines, Knots, Quarter Turns—Repeat

There is a field. Some say this is where memory resides, not in the body, nor hovering above the place where an action originally unfolded. Yet it goes where we go. To enter the field is to be in the midst of that which is imperceptible, incessant, without known origin, without end. But it can be changed. Does the hum still sound?

The Music of the Spheres
Sharifa Rhodes-Pitts

Straight Lines

.   .

.   .   .   .

.   .   ..

.   .   .

.   ..

.   .   ..

A

pinprick

gets

me.

..   ..

.   .   .

The bell of it punctuates the quiet—
                sharpens the focus by cleaving it.

                It rings out—directed, exact, its precision a
                small, resounding hammer. The bell sounds its
                distant noise—not a matted, muted friction,
                but a pinprick. It is a single point clarified and
                crystal. It is the single pin among the many, the
                pin of my sightline. I see it no matter where I'm
                standing, no matter how far away, I see it and
                then I hear the crisp bell of it. I still myself in
                anticipation of its ringing—let it pass through
                my body, slide over all of me. I still myself in
                the moment of its ringing and in the immediate
                aftermath. Because the bell sounds once, I know
                it can sound again and I wait for its total ringing.

How does the small sound, the little bell of me, shunt us along,
in a long, straight line, in all our slippery, soft language?
The bell clarifies the sound of the straight line, the solitary
focused sound of it—all the sounds become the one.

A straight line is a system to direct our focus, it is a narrow
but generous land bridge, pushing some material along—the
words charged as they are propelled along in logic, in sound,
in fortitude, in soft focus. A straight line builds in a chorus,
as accretion. It speaks in onblong minor chords—a hint of
something I thought I saw it glimmer in the margin.
        The chords converge, a requisite choir

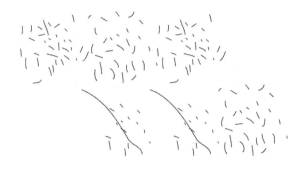

And now the line becomes a billowed volume,
two lines gather at their fine edges—the length
and breadth made visible. A pact forms between
the edges, we loosely bind the seams to make
them aware of one another.

Any single line becomes a line of sight, a desire
line—and my field of vision fans out into a soft
tributary.

    Meanwhile,

a foot presses the firm floor. A hand presses the firm floor. My
back on the firm floor—another foot on the floor, pressing
down, pushing along, aware of how the line has begun to billow.

    We press forward for new words,
    a tender line of words,
    soft focus stills itself to
    more of the same.
And before the words travel, there is the exacting pinprick. The
sound doesn't travel—it hovers and rings out. There is nothing

itinerant about it. The sound is a payload.

Held into the knot long enough, the words slip into a new place. The words eventually slip into a new place, become mere utterances, the words loosen their grip, are just outside of focus. Stare at anything too long and this happens. The sameness creates its own charged space, its own song, its everything. The sameness cuts a groove for a new space. It creates an effluence of sameness, an inundation of sameness—the rivulet of it.

Knots

The sound takes its texture, it claims it—takes all the quality of it and braids it. Threads it. It takes its makeup. Takes a shroud to encase it. Once inside, the shroud of sounds slip further, enter the middle of their entanglement

A knot is another kind of avowal, a covenant of we in language and limb. Take my hands and I will take your hands. We now have our hands, which lets us slip and stitch our words.

> With our hands like this
> we ready ourselves for the base of
> our language, choral and steadfast.

Or, call it a huddle—an acknowledgement that here we are, a baseboard, a soundboard, a tender turn. Every hand that is able to grip, grips. All the bells sound in the enclosure of the *we*. Their sounds are a knotted prophylactic. The mess of the

sounds fill me, slides all over me, creates a film, a steady peace
and disturbance.

.

.   .   .   .

.   .   ..

.   .   .

.   ..

.   .   ..

In a huddle we are knotted, limb for limb.
we, in the knot

The sound takes its texture, it claims it—takes
all the quality of it and braids it. Threads it. It
takes its makeup—beginning with the selvage,
ending nowhere. Takes the shroud and encases
it. The knot of sound presses and presses—it
can bear it.

Quarter Turns

For 1:00 pm to become itself, first we have to pass through
12:59 pm. We do. Inside of it, 60 seconds accrue. Small acts pass
inside the seconds. The acts cluster—second-long acts become
10 second acts and in accordance, the entire minute builds.

Sometimes, a referent reaches from the present minute to the
past, building for us an eloquent time bridge. What a tender
gesture, this small allotment. Seconds build to minutes and the
accumulated time slips softly from minute to minute.

1:00 pm becomes 1:01 pm, right past us.
1:01 becomes 1:02. 1:02 becomes 1:03 pm and
so on until the new time is 1:15 pm. Each minute
passes and 1:00 pm eventually becomes 1:15 pm.

Many small acts that have passed within that quarter hour,
that small turn of phrasal language. What a low, gliding hum.
Propulsion comes in a series of long, choral movements—
mistaken for no movement at all.

Four quarter turns equal a full rotation.

Repeat

．

．　　　　　　　　　．

．　　　　　．

．　　　．　　．．　　　　　．．

．．　　　　　　　　．

．　　　　　．　　　　　　．

．　　　　　　　　　　．．

．　　．　　...　　　　．

．

The pinprick gets me.
It got me.

．　　　　　．　　　　　　．

．　　　　　　　　　　　．．

．　　．　　...

What a prismatic longing, what a covenant. To speak to the
bloom. What bell, little tangle, what selvage that made us.

There is a room. There is an open door—call it invitational.
Remove the door from the hinges and call it a room that we
all fill. There is a low hum at the baseboard. The language
just on the other side of the door is one that you know. You
speak it and it rests inside of you. Bells and language mix so

that determined straight lines mix with knotted ones, mix with quarter turns—all our rightfully sliding language. The bell looks for a clean sound, one for all of us. It rings once and it may well ring again, so we hold for it. Meanwhile, we are knotted. Meanwhile, there is our rotation in words and gestures, we are knotted and tangled, we are shrouded, pressing on.

   .   .   ..

Acknowledgments

The title of this book, *No Knowledge Is Complete Until It Passes Through My Body*, comes from some ideas of Faustin Linyekula, which I read about in the piece "Faustin Linyekula: Remember His Name (and Country and Past)" by Brian Seibert published in the *New York Times* on September 5th, 2017. I read the article in advance of seeing Linyekula's piece "In Search of Dinozord" at the French Institute Alliance Française's Crossing the Line Festival in September 2017.

Éireann Lorsung welcomed me to Dickinson House in Olsene, Belgium for a fellowship during the summer of 2017. Many of the pieces that appear in this book took shape during my time at Dickinson House. Thank you, Éireann, for welcoming me and for creating that respite. Thank you also to Su Hwang and Arra Ross—we were all in residence together.

The Lower Manhattan Cultural Council has given me space on Governors Island, first through a Process Space residency in 2017 and then through an Artist Center of Governors Island residency in 2019-2020.

Many of the pieces in this book were written during two residencies at Danspace Project between 2019 and 2020. I was a writer-in-residence in the Voice & Body Research Group, which was convened in the months leading up to Danspace Project's PLATFORM 2020: Utterances from the Chorus (co-curated by Okwui Okpokwasili and Judy Hussie-Taylor). I was also a writer-in-residence for the PLATFORM 2020: Utterances from the Chorus. Thank you Judy Hussie-Taylor, Seta Morton, Lydia Davis, Okwui Okpokwasili, Jasmine Hearn, Tendayi Kuumba, Benedict Nguyen, Samita Sinha, and Tatyana

Tenenbaum for creating and sustaining the spaces for us to gather and think together.

Between October 2019 and March 2020, I was part of Okwui Okpokwasili and Peter Born's practice Sitting On a Man's Head. Sitting On a Man's Head was presented at Danspace Project as part of Danspace Project's PLATFORM 2020: Utterances from the Chorus. Okwui and Peter's process taught me more than I could imagine and I am grateful for the new ways they showed me how to be in conversation, inside a continuum, and in practice with others. Thank you also to all the other performer activators: Martita Abril, Jennifer Brogle, mayfield brooks, Leslie Cuyjet, André Daughtry, Eisa Davis, Brittany Engel-Adams, Lily Gold, Naja Gordon, Melanie Greene, Audrey Hailes, Remi Harris, Jasmine Hearn, Justin Hicks, Shayla-Vie Jenkins, Chaesong Kim, Tendayi Kuumba, Breyanna Maples, Priscilla Marrero, Anais Maviel, Maya Orchin, Kay Ottinger, jess pretty, Greg Purnell, Hans Rasch, Katrina Reid, Jean Carla Rodea, Lily Bo Shapiro, Samita Sinha, Eleanor Smith, Tatyana Tenenbaum, David Thomson, Pyeng Threadgill, Charmaine Warren, AJ Wilmore, Anna Witenberg, and Nehemoyia Young.

I return always to Loophole of Retreat, which Saidiya Hartman, Tina M. Campt, and Simone Leigh convened at the Guggenheim Museum on April 27, 2019. Thank you for bringing that day to life.

Thank you to everyone at Nightboat Books for continuing to publish the work that you do and thank you for making this book possible. Stephen Motika, Lindsey Boldt, Caelan Nardone, HR Hegnauer, and Jaye Elizabeth Elijah: I am so grateful for what you do.

And last but not least, thank you to Saint Ann's School for consistently supporting my work during these last six years, and in particular for the support during the summers of 2018 and 2019.

Thank you to the chorus of writers, artists, children I teach, places I've inhabited, and teachers who've taught me. There are now so many of you.

Thank you to the editors of the following journals and anthologies for originally publishing pieces that appear in *No Knowledge Is Complete Until It Passes Through My Body*:

"the order was in the hour of worship" originally appeared in *e-flux journal*, Issue #105, *Loophole of Retreat*, edited by Simone Leigh, Saidiya Hartman, and Tina M. Campt, December 2019.

"the honeybees invade the nunnery" appeared in *A Perfect Vacuum*, January 2020.

"the back door or the lone coast" and "L" appeared in *Columbia Review*, June 2020.

"quietude, gaped earth, substantial loss" published in *111O/10*, Fall 2018.

"on the structure of birds" and "A phoenix or again this ruin" (then titled "A phoenix justly transmutes ruin") appeared in *Chicago Review*, Issue 60:4, 2017.

"I reckon, a latitude" was published in *Bodies Built for Game: The Prairie Schooner Anthology of Contemporary Sports Writing*, edited by Natalie Diaz and Hannah Ensor, University of Nebraska Press, 2019.

"it was satisfactory" was published in *Makhzin, Issue 3: Dictationship*, 2018.

"if, after birth the border" and "concerning the house where I stayed December, 2017" appeared in *Black Sun Lit, VESTIGES_04: Aphasia*, 2019.

"atoll and archipelago" entries in *Counter-Desecration: A Glossary for Writing Within the Anthropocene*, edited by Marthe Reed and Linda Russo, Wesleyan University Press, 2018.

"at first, day one" appeared in the Poetry Project's *HOUSE PARTY #10*, May 2020.

"house series 5" was published in *Social Text Online* in October 2019.

An excerpt of "attention as a form of ethics" appeared in Academy of American Poets, Poem-a-Day, curated by Monica Youn, May 26, 2020.

Notes

- In the piece "the back door or the lone coast," the question "What kind of shape would you need to move 500 people quickly?" appears. This question is from a conversation between Christina Sharpe and Torkwase Dyson at the Graham Foundation, streamed live on June 14, 2018.

- The epigraph in "Part II: proviso for Asphodel Fields" comes from Lispector, Clarice. *The Hour of the Star.* Translated by Benjamin Moser, New Directions, 2011.

- "At first, day one" was written in conversation with Yoshiko Chuma's workshop "Shifting Concepts: from Poem to Body," which Chuma taught at the Poetry Project in March 2020.

- The word "subsisters" appears in "house series 5" and is borrowed from the title of Uljana Wolf's book, *Subsisters: Selected Poems*, (tr. Sophie Seita), published in 2018 by Belladonna* Collaborative.

Coda

L

after "O" by Claire Wahmanholm

long live our loyalty, how it loops, falls, lumbers, lulls and
lists—finally resisting its own limpness.

long live anything that has longwished to live: the lasso, the
lake, the limit, the left lane, the spices spinning on their lazy
susan. the lavender field at peak bloom, illustrious and ovenhot.
land and the outliers. land and the legion of the Outer Banks.
land and the landed. latitude and that was my limit until I
looked left. what length we expect to cover in these longitudinal
years, early loops sliced lengthwise to see their insides.

the latent exercise of the loom, left to right, layered weft and
warp listening to its language, leeched all across the living room.

an antecedent to loyalty is drift. drift or look away from the
limit. Let me look at the warped shapes inside the lava, angry
loaves lifting the mouth of the mountain then lifting clear off
the mountain. Leavened loaves at the limit of the leavening.
Left loaves rock hard obsidian thoughts make. My yearling,
even luxury has its limits. having lived or existed all year long.
love is a lifetime of long live our loyalty, how it loops, falls,
lumbers, lulls, and lists—finally resisting its own limpness. A
lifeline or ulna, all my limber bones held in my left hand. I have
placed the bones on a bay laurel wreath, placed the wreath
inside a barrel. lined up the barrel alongside other barrels laden
with laurels and ulnas. what to say of lavishing honor, what to
say of laconic, I once tried. what of leisure or lassitude.

Lateral pines loosen at the ends of their branches, languishing
before they fall, loop through the extra air. I am alone in
the lake region, algae bloom at my ankles loaves lifting the
mountain to make fresh archipelagoes.

Asiya Wadud is the author of *Crosslight for Youngbird*
(Nightboat Books, 2018), a finalist for the Hurston/Wright
Legacy Award in Poetry. Her other collections include *day pulls
down the sky / a filament in gold leaf*, written with Okwui
Okpokwasili (2019), *Syncope* (2019), and *No Knowledge
Is Complete Until It Passes Through My Body*. Asiya teaches
poetry at Saint Ann's School and is a member of the
Belladonna* Collaborative. Her work has been supported by
the Lower Manhattan Cultural Council, Danspace Project,
Foundation Jan Michalski, Brooklyn Poets, Dickinson House,
Mount Tremper Arts, and the New York Public Library, among
others. Asiya is a 2019-2020 Lower Manhattan Cultural Council
Artist-in-Residence and also a PLATFORM 2020: Utterances
from the Chorus (co-curated by Okwui Okpokwasili and Judy
Hussie-Taylor) writer-in-residence at Danspace Project. She
lives in Brooklyn, New York.

Nightboat Books

Nightboat Books, a nonprofit organization, seeks to develop audiences for writers whose work resists convention and transcends boundaries. We publish books rich with poignancy, intelligence, and risk. Please visit nightboat.org to learn about our titles and how you can support our future publications.

The following individuals have supported the publication of this book. We thank them for their generosity and commitment to the mission of Nightboat Books:

Kazim Ali
Anonymous (4)
Jean C. Ballantyne
The Robert C. Brooks Revocable Trust
Amanda Greenberger
Rachel Lithgow
Anne Marie Macari
Elizabeth Madans
Elizabeth Motika
Thomas Shardlow
Benjamin Taylor
Jerrie Whitfield & Richard Motika

In addition, this book has been made possible, in part, by grants from the National Endowment for the Arts, the New York City Department of Cultural Affairs in partnership with the City Council, and the New York State Council on the Arts Literature Program.